Being Animal

Being Animal

Poems by

Terri Glass

Cover design by Shay Culligan

ISBN: 978-1-952326-15-8

Kelsay Books
502 South 1040 East, A-119
American Fork, Utah, 84003

What is man without the beasts? If all the beasts were gone, men would die from great loneliness of spirit, for whatever happens to the beasts also happens to man.

–Chief Seattle
Suquamish and Duwamish

Acknowledgments

I am grateful to the editors of the following publications where these poems first appeared:

About Place, 2015: "Sea Stars" and "Wind Turbines of Altamont Pass"

Birdland Journal, 2019: "Waiting for the Lazuli Bunting"

Berkeley Public Library, *Poem in Your Pocket Day,* 2018 & 2019: "Where Did You Go?" "Absorb the night air," "Lightning quick fox" "It emerges" (haiku)

California Poets in the Schools, *Singing the Feathers of Freedom,* 2017: "Wood duck floats downstream" (haiku); 2018–2019, "Backyard Vista of the Bird Fiesta"

Finishing Line Press, 2015: *Birds, Bees, Trees, Love, Hee Hee* (haiku chapbook): "A bee drops," "Every morning"

Marin Poetry Center Anthology, 2018: "Puma"; 2019, "Spirit Bear"

Quiet Lightning, 2018: "The Bear that Reversed the Tale of Goldilocks"

San Diego Poetry Annuals, 2014: "River Keeper"; 2015: "Antelope Woman"; 2016: "The Pond People"; 2018: "Cow Tipping Tuesday"

Scarlet Tanager Press, 2018, *Fire and Rain; Ecopoetry of California:* "Wind Turbines of Altamont Pass"

The Fourth River, 2018: "Three weeks of rain" (haiku)

Vivace, 2009: "The Fox Path"; 2014: "Owl" and a version of "One Last Beauty"

Young Raven's Literary Review, Issue 6, 2017: "Violet Green Swallows"

I want to thank Claire Blotter, Margaret Stawowy and Rick Stanton for their editorial feedback on many of these poems. I would also like to thank my mentors in the Stonecoast MFA program: Cait Johnson, Barbara Hurd and Kazim Ali, who guided my exploration of poetry, prose and haiku that influenced some of this work.

Contents

Shifting

As Metaphor

Introduction

Being Animal is a collection of poems and haiku that represent many tiers of relationship to the animal world from a human and sometimes an animal perspective. My empathy and fascination with animals runs deep, and I often wonder what does human mean without the recognition of an animal presence inside us that mirrors the great diversity of all wildlife.

Some of these poems celebrate the beauty of animals or the longing to be one. Some represent the in-between place of animal and human form or the ability to shape-shift. One section addresses the difficulty of animals and humans coexisting. These relationships are not all harmonious; yet the wisdom, wildness and presence of animals continue to teach us we are of the earth, not separate from it.

We live in a culture that has dominated and destroyed many animal species, but I cannot imagine a world without honeybees, songbirds or frogs. Yet, due to human encroachment of unprotected habitats, we are experiencing the greatest loss of biodiversity since the Cretaceous period, 65 million years ago.

I hope *Being Animal* provides a bridge for more humans to appreciate and thus protect the species remaining on the planet.

Celebrating

Violet Green Swallows

Over Mount Burdell,
they flit, soar and dive
through a deep blue sky—
a glimpse of white belly
and dark green back
weaving among buckeye
in blossom and old live oak.
Skimming the sky,
dipping over my head,
may they anoint me
with levity
as I ascend the hill,
so my feet endure
jutting rocks and sudden dips
in the trail.

May their spirit fill
the troubled world
with joy—
visible angels not bound
by gravity or darkness.
Arrows of pure
freedom and play,
they dart about
catching insects,
currents of wind,
aerial circus acrobats.
Nimble, swift, I want
that gift to fly
among cumulus clouds,
and the blue
of blue-eyed grass sky.

I want everyone to feel
even for a moment—
the grace
of a violet green swallow.

Bee Remedy

April and the bees are in a tizzy
with wisteria spilling
perfume into the air.
Lavender flowers
cascade down the trellis
where underneath
I sit in a wicker swing
showered with blossoms.
I become the
surround sound of bees,
an orchestra of busyness.
I sense their purpose—
the hard work of nose-diving
into flower after flower.
What a life to fall into
Technicolor sweetness.
What a life to hum into existence
airy and driven and mad
about the flower kingdom,
a love affair we only
get a glimpse of
in our gravity dense bodies.

I am grateful for the work of bees
even though I have been stung.
Their little poison in my skin
is almost *honey* to my tongue.

Jackrabbit Wednesday

Out of the blue
one, two then three jackrabbits appear
from the grassy field,
onto the edge of the path
behind the reservoir filled with waterfowl.
They converge right in front of my friend and me,
one with ragged ears
two sniff each other, butt heads
and flee in opposite directions,
one headed toward me
like a locomotive;
ears luminous and large as a satellite dish
with spindly back legs, he sails on by
as if we were nonexistent.
We keep walking onward
to a bend in the path
where Clapper Rails wade in mud
at low tide.

The ragged-eared rabbit appears again
unafraid of our mammoth bodies
lumbering toward him.
He is doing his jackrabbit thing,
eating a bit of weedy grass,
sniffing the wind for something
sweet.

Spring at the reservoir
and I'm startled to catch
white paws flying into brush
every which way
among the usual visitors
of geese and pelicans.
I shout out to the wind,
there is no lack in my world
when it's Jackrabbit Wednesday!

Friday's Frog Chorus

Walking down the dirt path
next to a creek
filled with rainwater—
one frog croaks,
another calls back.
A ping-pong of sound
translates into my step,
a sound of pure happiness.
One frog croaks,
two more join in.
On and on,
a whole chorus of frogs
sing me into their world.
I am welcome without
being anyone in particular,
just a passerby
with old sneakers
and a floppy sun hat.
And what more could I want
in this world
than being a vessel
of reverberating sound—
a chime of frog chatter,
a roar of a rushing creek,
a gaggle of geese overhead.
What more could I want
on this Friday when the week
flew by in a series of missed
appointments with the Muse
than to find her here
alive in stereophonic
frog song?

Skink

It emerged from the
Cracker Jack box of the universe.
A crossword puzzle of lizard and snake,
sleek black body, neon blue tail
suddenly appearing
in the crevice of my patio.

Did Matisse dip that tail in paint?
And the way its body curled,
Dali could have made it his mustache.
Picasso with his twisted perspective
would have attached those sporty legs
to its snakelike body.

It feels like *Midnight in Paris*
where all the famous painters converge,
with the most edgy art
seeing the skink crawl along the stonework
whipping that blue tail around.

The Western Newt

The western newt
is so darn cute
with a face of E.T.
and a tail of a paddle,
it wiggles and scuffles,
squiggles and waddles
over fir needle ground.
With a coat of brown,
and a slender orange belly,
it has little webbed feet
squishy as jelly.
Don't give them a kiss—
you can't dismiss
their skin is toxic
like a pufferfish.

Waiting for the Lazuli Bunting

Hiking with a group of twenty
over Mount Burdell in spring,
everyone walking slower than me
stopping to view the boring wood peewee
or cryptic vireo.
The only reason I came—
to glimpse the stunning
lazuli bunting.
Bright as a bluebird,
smaller and more teal
with a cinnamon chest and milky belly,
rare as a clear agate
found in a dark wood.
every stop where the acorn woodpecker
flashed a bit of white on its wing,
every stop to listen
to the chipping sparrow's song,
I bit my lip,
but forged on.
Nowhere to pee,
nowhere to sit for lunch
but on a pile of thistle
and tick season at that—
I would not turn back.
I came to view the lazuli bunting.
On the very last trail
the park ranger heard its call,
nowhere to be seen among the buckeye and oak.
A house wren appeared in a tree's cavern
feeding its young,
so industrious and perky as a sprite.
I didn't care.
I came to view the lazuli bunting.

Backyard Vista of the Bird Fiesta

Ascend
Descend the golden-crowned sparrow,
The Oregon junco, the white-breasted nuthatch.
Surprise my eye oh spotted towhee
Descend the rain, the roots of oak.

Walk on down to the rising river
Way beyond the railroad tracks.
Quack the mallard in the slough
And a V of canvasback swims into view.

Ascend
Descend the California towhee,
The oak titmouse, the white-crowned sparrow.
Flit like a fly you skittish house finch,
Tip the birdfeeder bully scrub jay,
Descend the rain, the roots of oak.

Tromp my boots to the muddy hillside
Find windswept branches strewn about.
Whistle the robin in her habitat,
While an acorn woodpecker rat-a-tat-tats.

Ascend
Descend the chestnut-backed chickadee,
The downy woodpecker and mockingbird.
Scratch the leaf litter little fox sparrow,
Hang upside down you crazy nuthatch,
Scatter, zigzag, wild bird fiesta
Rejoice this winter solstice.

Five weeks of rain
standing water everywhere
happy happy frogs!

A bee drops
into a poppy's cup—
what a life!

It emerges
sleek as the waves it rolls with
river otter.

Animals in a Human World

Blue Whale at Bolinas

She lies there like a behemoth tube sock,
the surf rising up
then crashing down on her body.
No longer belonging to sea
but to sand and the hands
of the biologists who will carve
into her flesh
for a full necropsy.
Broken ribs,
blunt force trauma to her head.
Struck by a ship—wham.
Wrong place, wrong time.
The gentlest of beasts, an eater of krill
became road kill
by the busyness of ships
bringing in cargo from Japan.

Imagine the weight of a ship
barreling into a 79-foot whale.
And here on Agate Beach,
tiny stick figures called humans
scatter around her.
The waves roll in,
rinsing her great blue body
with sea foam,
singing her spirit back to sea.

Wind Turbines of Altamont Pass

Standing upright on barren hills
facing both sides of the freeway
catching the smog
spewing from automobiles
catching the wind in wild blades of steel
killing kestrels and red-tailed hawks
generating energy for power grids
lighting the streetlights of grimy alleyways
lighting the traffic light that turns red.
You stop breathless at these colossi
the loneliness of gray metal against blue sky
and ask what part of you
feels like this—
what part of your loneliness
churns thoughts inside your head,
kills the flight of your imagination
but lights the dark alleyways of your doubts?
What part of you
has hardened to your own spirit
longing to find the nearby delta
where egrets wade and rivers converge?
What part of you stands on barren hills
thrashing your arms toward the universe
hoping that all this thrashing
does some good in the world?

Sea Stars

As if fallen from the sky,
their five points illuminate
the bottom of the sea.
They have lived for centuries,
blood orange, deep purple
with perfectly symmetrical arms
now tearing off
and crawling away
from their bodies:
"sea star wasting syndrome."

Can you imagine what that feels like?

Maybe the bombing victims
of the Boston Marathon know
when that blast
left so many with shattered limbs.
Our nation severed
in so many directions.

The ocean now acid.

Today I found a tiny headless snake
squirming on my back patio. "What?"

I look at my body, still intact.
I love my arms
when they swoosh the summer air
as I hike up Mount Burdell.
The balance they create, the multitude
of purposes they serve.

Whole populations of sea stars
along the Pacific coast
vanishing like cities at night—
lights going out
one by one.

As their arms rip away
leaving their bodies in a limp mass,
I do my morning yoga, triangle pose,
my body five pointed.
My left arm vertical toward the sky
from where stars fall.

Sea Lions of Crescent City

They boost their blubbery bodies
up jagged rocks on the jetty
defying logic
and park themselves
near the Chart Room Restaurant.
A slumber party of sea lions
covers the entire sidewalk,
some drape themselves over
the picnic tables.

The docent at the mammal center
said they come for human interaction
or maybe food.
But they don't look at me curiously
as I come up close nor do they beg.
They just sleep
and squabble among themselves
with hoarse sea lion barks.

I wonder what draws sea lions
to the sidewalk.
The beach is close by and softer.
The ones in the sea flap
their flippers, rolling with the waves
looking utterly happy in their element.

Maybe they do come up for novelty,
I will never know.
When I scan the deep pools of their eyes,
I am lost in a world that is not mine.

Gopher Snake

Mary found it on her porch one day,
about a foot longer than a yardstick,
brown with patterned splotches.
For several years,
it kept the gophers and moles away
that unearthed her yard
in messy piles of dirt
breaking up her neat croquet lawn.
She welcomed the snake,
otherwise a startling visitor
and now the snake has left…

Many summer evenings
walking behind Mary's house
I have imagined a rattlesnake,
its neck cricked over
the swimming pool taking a sip,
and my eyes and step become alert
for any long and patterned
creature low to the ground.

Mary says she has never seen
a rattler here—
I feel somewhat relieved,
but I know the terrain,
they live here among the gopher snake,
the coons and coyotes.

You can say this is the hazard
of living in the country...
coons in your pantry, snakes on your porch,
skunks spraying underneath the house,
the smell entering my sleep
making me dream there was a gas leak.

A dead deer decaying behind the fence
creating an unnerving stench that lasted
for two weeks. A band of turkeys pooping
on the patio. A rat crawling into my
car engine and gnawing a hole in
my radiator hose.

And then there is
the harmless gopher snake
whom I never saw
who disappeared one day—
maybe killed by the gardener,
or slithered away to a neighbor's yard
quietly keeping pesky rodents in check.

The Bear that Reversed the Tale of Goldilocks

Driving along Eldorado Highway
from the eastern Sierras,
I stop at a country store
that replenishes hikers.
At the entrance stands
a wood carving of a 10-foot bear.

The shop owner in yellow t-shirt and shorts,
waits on me as I buy snacks,
expounds a tale of a black bear
that rambled right through front door
and chose a box of Lindor chocolates to eat.
What good taste, I thought of the bear.

The next story, the same bear
walks into the owner's house
behind the shop and gobbles down
a large Tupperware container of potato salad
without puncturing the plastic.
How courteous, I thought of the bear.

Final story, the bear meanders
into the owner's bedroom
and leaves a huge dump
on the carpet next to the bed
almost the size of elephant dung.
What a magnanimous conclusion, I thought of the bear.

Knickers, the Giant Steer

A hulk of Holstein mastery,
cows appear like midgets
swarming around his
black and white splotched
behemoth body.
He's tall as a pro basketball player,
enough meat on him to feed
a hundred, but too much girth
to fit him through
the slaughterhouse door.
So he wanders the field
on an Australian farm
grazing like a mowing machine.

We gawk at his hugeness,
wondering what it's like
to be that large—does he
feel mighty? Does he care
that he's a spectacle to the
human eye? A media hit,
a super freak,
a colossal hamburger factory,
but just too damn big to eat.

Of Mice and Maine

Inside the pinewood drawer
mice unravel threads
of my roommate's purple bra.

Chewing and chewing
the mice gnaw
through her new linen scarf.

Landlord sets four mousetraps
One in every room
Catch three.

Seven nights of this
my roommate hightails it
to a luxury hotel.

Graduation party tipsy,
I come home alone
into the dark cabin.

Under my high heel,
flattened like pizza crust
a baby mouse.

Cabbage worm sleeps
inside the crevice of my lettuce
I slice it in half.

28 years after Chernobyl
biggest problem
Colorado potato bugs.

Three weeks of rain
rat crawls into my car engine
for a little sauna.

Longing

Owl

(for Hazel)

The owl's eyes were so perfect, so black, so lustrous, so elliptical
that I wanted to be lost in them forever,
to enter into a bird's-eye view of the world,
to see in the dark, be the dark, be inside out blackness.

The owl's feathers were so gray, so gunmetal gray,
so coat-of-squirrel gray, so blue-gray
that I wanted neither day nor night,
to be in sheer limbo of it all, mute and silent.

The owl's head swiveled from left to right,
like it had no vertebra, like its head could twist off,
like watching a skater whip around in circles,
that I wanted all my thoughts to dissolve.

The owl's mottling was so white,
so virginal, like the soft down of a swan,
like a lamb lived in its feathers,
that I wanted to drift into deep sleep.

The spotted owl was so beautiful
that I no longer wanted to be human—
I wanted to dwell in the wellspring of those eyes,
take flight in the cool night air with fringed wings,
to be silent and soft feathered,
to fall from a great height at will
sensing the barely visible.

The Fox Path

I want to follow the fox path
and enter a different world
become swift, light-footed
wear an outrageous fur coat
aim like an arrow
toward my earthen home
dream fox dreams
in my hidden den
slip into the womb
of hibernation
melodic and serene
and always in tune
to the perfect hues of spring.
I want to follow the fox path—
the unknown beckoning
the ancient world of smell
the true field of touch—
paw to ground, nose to wind
fur radiating out
north, south, east and west.
I want to follow the fox path
and forget my humanness.
I want to follow the fox path
every morning I awake.

River Keeper

In downtown Martinez, California, a pair of beavers arrived in Alhambra Creek in 2006. The Martinez beavers built a dam 30 feet wide and at one time six feet high, and chewed through half the willows and other creek side landscaping the city planted as part of its $9 million flood-improvement project.

I want to be a beaver, a simple creature with two glassy black eyes and a spatula tail with which I whack the ground when I please. I want to gnaw down some rough-barked trees and jam a river, your river. I want to jam your river with logs, limbs and leaves. I want to waddle and jam and slap and mow. I want to mow down a forest full of willows with my big chunky teeth and let my olive-sized nostrils whiff the aspen breeze.

I just want to be a beaver, not your beaver, a beaver. With mud and stone in my forepaws and timber between my teeth, I want to build a six-foot high dam that dazzles muskrats and minks. I want to outflank the Army Corps of Engineers and infiltrate every river, stream and creek.

I want the handsome fur coat that, no, you cannot pet. And live in a den underwater that's not a welcome habitat for any wishful human to probe, poke or peer.

I want to build a bridge between waterways with logs of birch. When I waddle, I want my underbelly to scrape the detritus of earth. I want to string the seasons into some kind of thatch, a seal from winter storms where I languidly rest.

I want to be a beaver, with a thick fur pelt and a bouquet of stiff whiskers. I want to go my beaver ways and not be bothered by fishing line or tack. I want to gnaw, whittle and whack. And build build build up that pile of sticks to block out your scent: you musky human, with your lures and animal traps.

Swan and Drought

I am defined by blue,
blue sky, blue water.
Cloud white I am, once
a cloud floating on water.

I circle and circle
the summer sky
looking for the still blue pond—
gone.

I long to float on water
to feel the coolness seep
beneath my feathers,
my body buoyant as air itself.

I am tired circling this sky.
I want the rain to slide
underneath my translucent wings,
to rest on the pond
nestling my beak into my soft body.

Seasons pass. No water.
How long can I be a cloud
empty of rain? How long can the sky
hold only white clouds?

Hungry for Company

They scatter and scurry
like a flurry of snow in midwinter
as I flush quail up from a dusty path.
But it is midsummer at Rush Creek
and no other animals are out and about.
Where are the pelicans or egrets
that convened for a mass convention of white
in this marsh last week?
No scrawny coyotes in the surrounding hills
or mule deer feeding in the tall blond grass.
I scan the terrain like a hungry mountain lion,
but I am only hungry for company.
Just me, and the scattering quail,
me and the incoming fog
as I pick up my pace
circumnavigating my aloneness.

Bluebirds

I became a Bluebird at age 6, with a little navy cap
emblazoned with a bluebird, a red vest,
navy A-lined skirt. I loved this uniform,
and belonging to a league of girls
whose pledge was to have fun,
learn to make beautiful things,
learn about nature and living outdoors,
to make friends.

Never saw a real bluebird
until five decades later
on top of Ring Mountain. A small bird flitting
low to the ground. A thrill to view a bird
neither yellow nor brown.
Neither turquoise nor indigo, but cobalt blue,
a jewel of blue with a citrine chest.
A jewel of sky. Walking with a man
I deeply loved, the air of bluebirds
emblazoned my heart with greater joy.
I wore a cap of happiness, the vest of hope.

My bluebird girl, winged, full of wonder
grew up and wrote poems
about a secret love affair
with visits rare as the bluebirds themselves.
But the time spent together felt eternal—
entering the ethers of another world.

Waiting for the bluebirds to return,
I stand on Ring Mountain in spring
making friends with sparrows and warblers.
But oh, the memory of blue floods my eyes
and my heart opens like a field of wild lupine.

One Last Beauty

I want the world to come to me
with yellow daffodils
and white butterflies
or a serving of chocolate crème brûlée
on a porcelain plate
while I sit on the sun porch
reading Wordsworth
and flipping through a book of art
by Matisse.
I want a dark handsome man
to gently brush my hair away
as he kisses the nape of my neck
and unbuttons the back of my dress.

I don't want the news of yet another
polar bear drowning
as the ice caps melt,
or stories of mutated frogs
with legs growing out of their stomachs,
or the report of 4000
red-winged blackbirds dropping dead
from the sky on New Year's Eve.
Please spare me the fact
of the colony collapse of honeybees.

Bring me news
a field of daffodils may bring.
Show me the blue sky of hope
after the acid rain.
Show me the resiliency
of that brilliant last cricket
who sings its song
after all other creatures are gone.

Every morning
the lone goose calls—
where is its mate?

Deadlines—
how I long for evening
laced with cricket song.

Overhead gray sky
a stream of geese honking—
my restless heart.

Shifting

First Feathers

There is an ache in my bones
old as the Cretaceous.
I am part dinosaur, winged and reptilian
crushed, fossilized
in the strata of earth.
My vertebrae lodged in limestone.
My tail an imprint of first feathers—
a desire to fly over seas
of writhing creatures who rise
and snap with great jaws
as I leap and lift off
by a w i n g s p a n of invention.
I am part bird,
trapped in stone
asleep for millions of years.
This bird bears weight in my bones.
She is my phylogeny, my alphabet of history,
the *edge* of evolution.
Rising to the surface,
she wakes me
by the thrum of her wings.

Puma

Moondrop eyes,
paws of steel—
you
who roam the hills
near home,
silent, stealthy,
invisible to prey
until you
pounce.
Runner of wind, of time,
you traverse miles like
liquid amber
flashing through autumn grass,
paw prints
disappearing in dust,
your breath aflame.
Your heartbeat, a compass
mapping your terrain.
Closest ancestor
to my wildness,
you prowl
inside my soul
forcing me alert
and to hunt
any small rustle or scent
that leads me toward
that edge
of aliveness.

The Pond People

Crawling out of the pond
with their webbed feet,
they know the ways of ducks,
the calls of Canada geese,
the stone silence of frogs.
They can stand for hours on one leg
like a great blue heron
and long to have the wingspan of a harrier
to glide over nearby fields.
They wince at the click of camera shutters:
so they come out before daylight
and retreat before seen.
But I have seen them. I know who they are.
More delicate than creatures of the Black Lagoon,
they are part dream, part myth,
more real than my ten fingers and toes.
They are the pond people who know
the water world. They are our ancestral blood.
And if you wake up early enough,
you may catch a small movement
from the corner of your eye.
Look at your feet—
have they been blessed with algae?
Can you feel the shaft of a feather
piercing your skin?

Antelope Woman

I smell sage and dust,
scan the tan desert light.
My shins, the branches of willow,
my hooves, the nubby stubs of chalk
as I thud over rough terrain.

My deep brown eyes mirror dusk.
If you enter them, you will be lost
in the forest of tomorrow.

Come run with me.
Run with my band, my portable village
of antelope people.
Run away from the storm brewing
in the thundering black skies,
run away from the two-footed creatures
who plant wheat and carry weapons.

Snake Woman

She shed her limbs
so her sleek body
moved like an undulating wave.
She shed her skin
and glowed like a wild flame.
She sunned herself on rocks,
and her warmth gathered like
the swelling tide.
She spoke with a forked tongue
only to mirror the duplicitous world
then polished her fangs
to cut through patriarchal lies.

She never left the garden
where the shake shake shake
of her rattle was *not* a warning,
but became the rhythmic pulse
to the greatest song on Earth.

Spirit Bear

In my dream,
I am like Tarzan's Jane,
half-clothed, running
through the dense forest
when a baboon
takes a shine to me
with its toothy grin.
I keep running.
A huge white bear appears,
eyes me like I'm
a blonde in a bar.
I succumb to its wiles.
The bear mounts me
missionary style,
his sheath revealing
a pink red penis.
The sex igniting me
like 1000 buzzing bees.
I take on Spirit Bear's energy,
catching more salmon
than any black bear,
outrunning fox and coyote,
swimming faster than sea wolf.

How can I return
to the human world
now that the wild
rages inside of me?

The Wren in My Head

Ekphrastic poem from Thomas Terceira's "Metamorphosis 2"

The wren in my head
tapped three times
so the map of my body
became a bird with black wings
that flew over a new world.

The wren in my head
tapped three times
so my imagination
opened to a future alive
with forests of flying squirrels.

The wren in my head
tapped three times
so my tightly built nest
on ground would endure
a great sea flooding the shore.

The wren in my head
tapped three times
so the map of my body
seeded earth to burst forth
in blossom after blossom after blossom.

Absorb the night air
move into animal presence
hoo-hooo, hoo-hooo, hoooo.

Lightning quick fox
I follow until I wear
a plush coat of rust.

No time for thought
be the softness of lambs wool
gently bleat to sleep.

As Metaphor

Where Did You Go?

Crow, crow where did you go?
Your black cloak does not hang
in my closet.

Dove, dove where did you fly?
Your olive branch does not fit
my mouth.

Duck, duck where did you swim
when the pond in my heart
froze over?

Squirrel, squirrel where did you hide
now that my branches
are bare?

Fox, fox who did you hunt
when my footprints disappear
in the snow?

Crow, crow where did you go?

The Shape of Seagulls

All facing the sea,
a fortress of seagulls stretches over the sand.
Their dark gray plumage
mimics the low-hanging fog.
I walk straight up to their citadel,
a divider where beach dwellers lie.

Squawk squawk squawk
walk waddle walk
Squawk squawk

I cannot face them flying away,
they look so cozy nuzzled up,
all 1000 of them.
I turn back.
But my first instinct, break up their fortress
just like I love to crush oak balls.
Because I have a 13-year-old boy inside me,
challenging the status quo,
because there is a fire inside me that wants
my world to explode in a new direction—
not a division of a two-party system,
not a he-said she-said,
but something fierce and fed by
a larger shape of the soul,
a startling movement,
a V of pelicans flying over the sea,
an arch of dolphins leaping out of the water
orchestrated by the truth of moonlight.

So Many, the Numbers

I will never forget the late fall day
we drove up the Nooksack River
full of spawning salmon.
Surprised to catch a few eagles
feasting on the ground,
then our eyes lifted to the tall firs,
where over *one hundred* perched.
Heads white as ghosts,
beaks fierce as scythes.
All feathers and talons,
wingspan and visual acuity.
Never had I seen so many
bald eagles in one place,
and the vast number of salmon
zeroing upstream.

This is what the earth looked
like 40 years ago,
before cell phones,
the internet, 7 billion people,
the melting ice caps.
This was my panorama
when my future was fresh
and the world full of promise:
silvery salmon, wild rivers
our national emblem
visible to the eye,
the great shriek to freedom!

Now my panorama is
a large-screen TV blaring
thousands of immigrants
fleeing Honduras,
overheated, underfed

marching toward
a militia-lined border in
America.

The eagle, only a memory
circling overhead.
Freedom—
a phantom cry.

Wapiti

Laden with antlers of eight tines,
burly chest with shaggy mane,
legs that outrun coyote,
the bull elk strides across hills,
the grand sentinel protecting
a harem of cows and young
grazing on native grasses.

I call out their real name: wapiti
meaning white rump.

They number 500 now
on Point Reyes Peninsula.
Nearly extinct from overhunting
for hide and tallow,
one last herd was brought back
by a southern rancher
and the tule elk multiplied.

Each winter,
males shed their antlers
giving back bone to the earth.
Each spring the cows give birth.
Each autumn, the bull bugles,
the call
high pitched, ascending,
the human version of
Brando screaming "Stella."

Animal of declaration,
ornamentation, strength.
Wapiti, wapiti, wapiti.
May your real name
echo through these hills.

May your bugle awaken us
to follow our own heart's desire.
May we carve out that path
just as your hooves wear a trail
over this rocky peninsula.

Road Trip

Driving down 101 near Laytonville,
I see the most ridiculous thing
in the opposite lane, a llama trotting
with a string of cars behind it,
head held high like a camel
leading a caravan through a desert.
Dear llama, who do you belong to?
Although I don't blame any animal
that wants to take off on its own road trip.

My boyfriend and I did
when we abruptly left college mid-quarter,
piled into a red '64 VW bug
and headed for the Southwest
hoping to join a commune somewhere.
Midway to Arizona, we stopped in Reno,
got married in an Elvis chapel
to the horror of our parents and continued
on 'til we reached the Painted Desert.
We were in awe of the geology:
buttes, alluvial fans, petrified rock.
Statues of saguaro cactus
welcomed us like sanctioned priests,
and the blue of the Southwest sky
ripped open the top of our heads.

We were rambling escapees from academia
loving our freedom like the llama,
which is not ridiculous after all,
just a bit startling
like our own wild impulses
sending us down an unknown highway.

Bobcat

Broad daylight
right in front of my car
bobcat hightails it
across the suburban street
tufted ears, cropped tail
hind legs bounding
into brush,
a wild card thrown in front of me.

Bobcat medicine says
look for what is hidden—
not all is as it appears to be.
Trust your own gut.

Bobcat, where are you going?
Are you chasing a jackrabbit
I cannot see?

Jackrabbit medicine says
plan for possibilities,
do not box yourself into
a corner. Make quick
and rapid turns if need be.

I turn the car.
Bobcat disappears.
All I have is a memory
of its movement,
its message stamped
on my forehead
as I gun the gas pedal
headed toward the
unmarked intersection.

Hiking Drakes Beach at 60

Overhead the sky hung heavy and gray.
Sand slid beneath my hiking boots
as I walked past columns of sandstone
that rose 120 feet or more
with horizontal striations thousands of years old.
The cliffs were as colorless as the sky
and my feet wore thin with fatigue
as I zigzagged over several streams
created from the incoming tide,
maneuvering between dry and wet sand
past piles of broken shells, pebbles
and sea plants battered by the waves.
The bones in my feet felt as old as the cliffs.

Before I reached Estero Bay,
one sea lion pup with his flippers
flounced and flopped toward the ocean
then dove into the waves.
Ah, for one brief moment,
buoyancy as I watched the seal pup
rise and fall in the surf.
For one brief moment I was 11 again
when nothing was gray
and my body bounded with energy.

I looked down the beach,
just a little further to trudge on
where a string of white pelicans
marked the edge of an inlet
opposite a station of black cormorants.

Cow Tipping Tuesday

Back from the store with a tote bag
slung on both shoulders,
one heavier than the other
full of bottled tea,
my body tips to the right.
I am waddling like an old cow,
one false step and I splat on the sidewalk.
I feel rather bovine these days,
slow moving, placid,
and I fear someone will put me out
to pasture—if not myself.

If I fell asleep in a field standing up
surely a group of mischievous teens
could tip me over,
my belly exposed to the night sky
with my legs stiff as cardboard.
Instead I find myself nodding off
on the couch around nine,
no good to the outside world,
my brain sifting through the day's events,
one of waiting in line
single file at Safeway to buy tea
to keep me awake in day
to crank out a poem or two.

A Poet Reflects on Stillness

There is all this morning light,
because I've given up the fight
to claw my way to the top.

I put myself out to pasture,
and all I hear is the laughter
of birdsong and jackrabbit hop.

In stillness vastness abounds,
cougar stalks the hills without sound—
chatter of squirrel finally stops.

Dragonflies dancing
over meditation pond
I step lightly on stones.

Wood duck floats downstream
As I lay in the hammock
I drift with the clouds.

Heaven on earth—
being me
being animal.